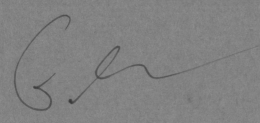

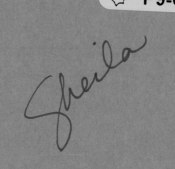

Sheila

Lynda

Dory

Kathin

Have You Filled a Bucket Today?

A Guide to Daily Happiness for Kids

By Carol McCloud

Illustrated by David Messing

Ferne Press

Author's Dedication

I dedicate this book to my late sister-in-law, Elizabeth Walsh, and to all other bucket fillers around the world. Liz had a wonderful way of affirming all people. Her encouraging words lifted our spirits and helped us to do more than we thought possible. Liz died suddenly, in the prime of life, as I was writing this book.

Author's Acknowledgments

In the 1960's, Dr. Donald O. Clifton (1924-2003) first created the "Dipper and Bucket" story that has now been passed along for decades. Dr. Clifton later went on to co-author the *#1 New York Times* bestseller *How Full Is Your Bucket?* and was named the Father of Strengths Psychology.

My deepest gratitude to Dave Messing, who put hours of heart, soul and creativity into each illustration; to the Nelson Publishing & Marketing crew; to my alternate editor and eight-year-old niece, Karley Walsh; to Mike McCloud, my husband and ever-present supporter of twenty-four years, who died a few months after this book was first published; and to the Lord my God, who leads me from within and has prompted me to one day write a sequel with Him in it.

A portion of the proceeds from this book is being donated to the Salvation Army, an organization that for more than one hundred years has served and modeled love and compassion for others.

McCloud, Carol.
Summary: The concept of bucket filling is an effective metaphor for encouraging kind and considerate behavior and for teaching the benefits of positive relationships.

ISBN # 978-1-933916-16-3
I. McCloud, Carol. II. Have You Filled a Bucket Today?: A Guide to Daily Happiness for Kids
Library of Congress Control Number: 2007936273

FERNE PRESS

Ferne Press is an imprint of Nelson Publishing & Marketing
366 Welch Road, Northville, MI 48167
nelsonpublishingandmarketing.com
(248) 735-0418

Introduction by Carol McCloud

I first learned about bucketfilling in a parenting workshop at an early childhood conference in the 1990's. The speaker, an expert in infant brain research, said it is helpful to think of every baby as being born with an invisible bucket. The bucket represents a child's mental and emotional health. You can't see the bucket, but it's there. She went on to say that it is primarily the parents' or other caregivers' responsibility to fill a child's bucket. When you hold, caress, nurture, touch, sing, play and provide loving attention, safety and care, you fill your child's bucket. Yes, we all know that babies require love. Giving love fills buckets.

However, in addition to being loved, children must also be taught how to love others. Children who learn how to express kindness and love lead happier lives. When you love and care about others and show that love with what you say and do, you feel good and you fill your own bucket too.

This book was written to teach young children how to be bucket fillers. As you read this book with children, use it as an opportunity to model bucketfilling by filling their buckets. Tell them why they are special to you. Help them think about what they might say or do to fill someone else's bucket. Work with your children and help them practice daily bucketfilling. Very quickly they will experience the pride and joy of filling buckets. Happy bucketfilling!

For more information on youth and adult presentations, books and other products or to receive our free e-newsletter, BUCKET FILL-OSOPHY 101, visit www.bucketfillers101.com.

If you enjoyed this book, you will also enjoy our prequel, *Fill a Bucket: A Guide to Daily Happiness for Young Children*. This book is written for parents and children from birth to age eight.

Carol McCloud, Author

All day long, everyone in the whole wide world walks around carrying an invisible bucket.

You can't see it, but it's there.

You have a bucket.
Each member of your family has a bucket.

Your grandparents, friends, and neighbors all have a bucket.

Everyone carries an invisible bucket.

Your bucket has one purpose only.

Its purpose is to hold your good thoughts and good feelings about yourself.

You feel very happy and good
when your bucket is full,

and you feel very sad and lonely
when your bucket is empty.

Other people feel the
same way, too.

They're happy when their buckets are full
and they're sad when their buckets are empty.

It's great to have a full bucket
and this is how it works . . .

You need other people to fill your bucket
and other people need you to fill theirs.
So, how do you fill a bucket?

You fill a bucket when you show love to someone, when you say or do something kind, or even when you give someone a smile.

That's being a bucket filler.

A bucket filler is a loving, caring person who says or does nice things that make others feel special.

When you make someone feel special, you are filling a bucket.

But, you can also dip into a bucket and take out some good feelings. You dip into a bucket when you make fun of someone, when you say or do mean things, or even when you ignore someone.

That's being a bucket dipper.

A bully is a bucket dipper.

A bucket dipper says or does mean things
that make others feel bad.

Many bucket dippers have an empty bucket.
They think they can fill their own bucket
by dipping into someone else's . . .
but that will never work.

You never fill your own bucket when you dip into someone else's.

But guess what . . .
 when you fill someone's bucket,
  you fill your own bucket too!

You feel good when you help others feel good.

All day long, we are either filling up or dipping into each other's buckets by what we say and what we do.

Try to fill a bucket and see what happens.

You love your mom and dad. Why not tell them you love them?
You can even tell them why.

Your caring words will fill their buckets right up.

Watch for smiles to light up their faces. You will feel like smiling too. A smile is a good clue that you have filled a bucket.

If you practice, you'll become a great bucket filler.

Just remember that everyone carries an invisible bucket,
and think of what you can say or do to fill it.

Here are some ideas for you.
You could smile and say "Hi!" to the bus driver.

He has a bucket too.

You could invite the new kid at school to play with you.

You could write a thank-you note to your teacher.

You could tell your grandpa that you like to spend time with him.

There are many ways to fill a bucket.

Bucket filling is fun and easy to do.
It doesn't matter how young or old you are.
It doesn't cost any money.
It doesn't take much time.

And remember, when you fill someone else's bucket,
you fill your own bucket too.

When you're a bucket filler, you make your home, your school, and your neighborhood better places to be.

Bucket filling makes everyone feel good.

So, why not decide to be a bucket filler today and every day?
Just start each day by saying to yourself,

"I'm going to do something to fill someone's bucket today."

And, at the end of each day, ask yourself,
"Did I fill a bucket today?"

"Yes I did!" That's the life of a bucket filler . . .

And that's YOU!

About the Author

Carol McCloud, the Bucket Lady, is a popular speaker in schools, churches, community groups, and business organizations. As an early childhood specialist and educator, Carol understands that patterns of self-esteem start very early in life and are fostered by others. Carol is president of Bucket Fillers, Inc., an educational organization in Brighton, Michigan dedicated to improving the quality of lives. For more information, visit www.bucketfillers101.com.

About the Illustrator

After graduating from Wayne State University in Detroit, Michigan, with a split major of advertising design and sculpture, Dave Messing started cartooning for youth-oriented magazines. Dave, his wife Sandy, and their boys Scott, Kevin, and Adam, have taught in their family-owned art school, Art 101, for twenty-five years. Dave also designs and builds props and miniatures for film and print commercials. You have seen his work on TV and billboards and in national magazines and movies. His client list ranges from historical museums to Harley-Davidson to almost every car manufacturer. He enjoys teaching and all forms of art from sculpture to cartooning.